John S. Blue

HOOSIER WIT & WISDOM

By *JOHN S. BLUE*

Sketches By Dale Fleming

Printed by Thomson-Shore, Inc.
Dexter, Michigan

Graphics and Special Art Work
by Huron Valley Graphics, Inc.
Ann Arbor, Michigan

The Hoosier then, what is he? His character is not easy to describe, for he is a compound of many contradictory qualities. He is both sentimental and shrewd, provincial and sophisticated, suspicious and generous, nosey and self-contained, quick-tempered and kind, self-righteous and tolerant, egotistical and unpretentious.

—William E. Wilson

Everybody says that the Hoosier is and always will be different from other people.

—Thomas R. Marshall

You can tell I'm an Indiana boy. There's somethin' about a fella from Indiana. I don't know what it is. Well . . . I do know what it is, but I don't like to think about it.

—Herb Shriner

Acknowledgements

A number of people have contributed in several ways in the preparation of the manuscript for this small volume, including, but not limited to, research, proof-reading, correction and arrangement. Appreciation for this kind assistance is therefore extended to Sarah Blue, Helen G. Brown, Richard A. Busse, William F. Campbell, H.R. Caniff, Shirley S. DeWees, John R. Funk, James A. Hankins, Marvin L. Ham, Jr., John R. Jeffers, Robert C. Kriebel, Mary K. Martin, Richard S. McGaughey, William J. Moriarty, Jr., Barbara T. Newcombe, Frank B. Schantz, Jr., Melinda J. Schantz, Susan Schreibman, Sharon Schulenberg, James R. Suelzer, Betsy Vanable, John W. Wixon, Willis J. Wright and Ethel M. Yoder.

Special Introduction

Indiana is a goldmine, filled with rivers and lakes; plains and hills of soft, warm beauty; and of beautiful and ingenious people. The famed professional basketball star George McGinnis once told how much he hated leaving Indianapolis for Philadelphia because "Indiana is like one big family to me."

Author John S. Blue has that feeling, too; and in "*Hoosier Wit and Wisdom*" he digs and pans it into a string of gem-like profiles of long departed brothers.

Throughout these mini-biographies runs the central theme of what makes great Hoosiers great. They all have a willingness to work and to change with the times. They possess a certain unflashy confidence. They were born with a feel for human nature. They mined and refined a rich vein of humor.

There are simply not enough books like this around, glorifying in the permanence of print the human treasures that have been, and will go on being, our Hoosier heritage.

Thank goodness John Blue has seen the treasure, and the prospects, and has gone about mining it for us all.

— Robert C. Kriebel, Editor
Lafayette Journal and Courier
Lafayette, Indiana

Contents

1 GEORGE ADE   1

2 KENESAW MOUNTAIN LANDIS   15

3 JOHN ADE   25

4 JAMES WHITCOMB RILEY   31

5 JAMES E. WATSON   47

6 LEW WALLACE   63

7 JACOB PIATT DUNN   69

8 JOHN T. McCUTCHEON   77

9 THOMAS RILEY MARSHALL   91

10 HERB SHRINER   103

11 GABRIEL GODFROY   119

12 ELBERT M. ANTRIM   125

SKETCHES BY DALE FLEMING

George Ade	preceding 1
Kenesaw Mountain Landis	14
Indiana General Store	18
John Ade	24
James Whitcomb Riley	30
The Riley Tree	35
James E. Watson	46
Lew Wallace	62
Jacob Piatt Dunn	68
John T. McCutcheon	76
Thomas Riley Marshall	90
Herb Shriner	102
Gabriel Godfroy	118
Elbert M. Antrim	124

Preface

It is a rather sad fact that a preface is not carefully read, if at all, since it is the only personal contact between the author and the reader. It affords an opportunity for the author to reveal how the book came to be written and what purpose it was intended to serve, if not readily apparent to the reader from its contents. Reading it may only amount to the reader unconsciously paying tribute to the author for the long, tedious hours of research, many times fruitless, and agonizing over its composition.

The initial selections were compiled for personal enjoyment only from the countless books written about famous Hoosiers, of little remembered quotations and human interest stories that appeared to be as fresh, humorous and relevant today even though time has dulled a general interest in, and knowledge of, their lives and accomplishments. An additional incentive for doing so stemmed from the personal recollection of having met three of these famous Hoosiers: George Ade, Kenesaw Mountain Landis and former U.S. Senator, James E. Watson.

In the process of adding other selections, the

idea of publication first occurred from the impact of discovering interesting source material, not even being sought, that seemed not to be a mere coincidence. Eventual publication was induced when all reasons advanced for not doing so were swept aside by an impelling belief that such a book as this would warrant publication, would be read more than once, and would not likely be soon discarded.

That the subjects are dominated by authors and politicians was not entirely a matter of chance. R.E. Banta, author of *Hoosier Caravan* points out: "Observers agree that Hoosiers have two marked characteristics: an over-weaning desire to see themselves in print and an uncontrollable appetite for politics."

That writers comprise the greatest number is borne out by research showing a predominate number to be Hoosiers. Howard H. Peckham, author of *Indiana a Bicentennial History* states: "When the perennial Chautauqua lecturer the late Opie Read first appeared in Fort Wayne, he announced that he was aware of Indiana's literary reputation and therefore, if there was an author in the audience, would he please stand. Whereupon the audience rose, en masse. Mr. Read recovered himself in time to notice one old man still seated and called attention to him as one Hoosier who was *not* an author. 'Oh, no, he writes too,' someone said. 'He's just deaf and didn't hear the question.' "

One

GEORGE ADE (1866–1944), noted Hoosier journalist, author and playwright, was born at Kentland, Indiana. He graduated from Kentland High School and Purdue University. His career as a writer began in 1890, when at the urging of a fellow Purdue student, John T. McCutcheon, he moved to Chicago to be employed as a reporter for the Morning News (later the News-Record, and then the Record).

His success as a reporter soon earned him the unrestricted opportunity to employ his perceptive talents as a daily columnist. A later collection of stories from this column, "Stories of the Streets and of the Town" comprised initial publication of Fables in Slang published in 1899. While two other books containing stories from his daily column were previously published, Fables in Slang brought him national prominence as an author.

1

In 1902 he acquired 417 acres of farm land east of Brook, Indiana, at a point where present Indiana Highway No. 16 crosses the Iroquois River. This became Hazelden, his country estate. In 1904 he erected a beautiful Tudor style residence (now a National Historic Landmark) at the edge of "a grove of century-old oaks." Hazelden was afterwards the site of numerous public meetings and historic celebrations. Here, in 1908, William Howard Taft, nominated as President opened his campaign. General Charles G. Dawes, nominated as Vice-President in 1924 made his closing campaign speech at Hazelden.

Notable persons from all over the country came to Hazelden to pay their respects or to be entertained as his guest. No Hoosier could claim the acquaintance and friendship of more famous people than George Ade. Just their names and a brief description of each, would fill a small volume. To name but a few: James G. Blaine, William Jennings Bryan, Will Rogers, Grover Cleveland, Calvin Coolidge, Admiral George Dewey, Kenesaw Mountain Landis, Mark Twain, James Whitcomb Riley, Theodore Roosevelt, Booth Tarkington and Douglas McArthur. Ade obviously had a wealth of untold stories about his own life and his association with the famous people of his day. One is led to believe that had he written a final book of his recollections it would have survived his many published works.

2

The following selections have been compiled from a biography written by Fred C. Kelly and published after Ade's death, and from miscellaneous related sources.

*H*E DEVELOPED an avid following of his column, "Stories of the Streets and of the Town." They were very simple stories about ordinary people, places and situations. One concerned an account of a distressed customer complaining to the clerk in a store on return of a hat that he said did not fit. The clerk replied, "Neither do your clothes." Another related the plight of a visitor being chased by an inmate in an insane asylum. As he was overtaken by the maniac he "felt a hand on his back and a voice close to his ear saying, 'You're it! You're it! Now see if you can catch me!' "

AS A YOUNG newspaper reporter in Chicago he had the rare opportunity to interview Col. Robert G. Ingersoll, "the most openly denounced and most secretly admired person in the United States." Years later in recalling this interview he told of his boyhood interest in Ingersoll's lectures "printed in cheap pamphlet form" which "had to be bootlegged and never were read in the house—always in the haymow. We loved them. They gave us the goose pimples. Bob was defying and flaunting all the preachers and hard moralists and Sunday school tyrants and we had a terrified admiration for him because he was sassing the people who kept us locked in for so many pleasant Sabbaths and who had crushed our spirit of research. . . ."

ADE COVERED the Columbian Exposition in Chicago in 1893 in a column entitled, "All Roads Lead to the World's Fair." One of the stories that did not get published related to the opening ceremony and review of a parade by President Grover Cleveland and Daniel S. Lamont, Secretary of War. It was a cold day in May. As they stood on the platform a member of the welcoming committee approached with two glasses of strong beverage saying, "I thought possibly you might want something to warm you up." The President replied, "Lamont doesn't use this stuff"—and poured the two into one!

FOLLOWING publication of his book, *Artie,* George Ade became a member and later president of the Forty Club in Chicago. This resulted in his acquaintance with the club's chaplain, Rev. Ernest Stires, later to become Rector of St. Thomas Episcopal Church in New York. Ade said, "To be with him was almost enough to induce a man to attend church and try to lead a better life."

HIS PARENTS, John and Adaline (Bush) Ade, lived to witness his national prominence as a writer and his phenomenal financial success. In their later years he entertained them in New York. At one time during their stay at the Herald Square Hotel, in deference to his distinguished guest, the head clerk struck up a friendly conversation in the hotel lobby with John Ade by inquiring if this was his first visit to New York. When informed that he had been there once before, the clerk asked if he had noticed any changes. He replied, "Oh, yes. Indeed I do! The town is considerably larger. Quite a number of new buildings have been put up. As I go around I observe ever so many improvements. There's no question about it, this town has changed." The clerk then inquired how long it had been since he was there, to which he casually replied, "Seventy-two years."

HE ONE TIME WROTE that he "firmly believed in short words and short sentences." However he departed from this rule in a classic tribute and description of his mother: "Her willingness to serve and help and comfort was so unbounded and her goodness was so efficiently directed by unruffled common sense and entire lack of theatrical emotionalism that sometimes I marvel at the fact that, from no merit of my own, I was privileged to have such a remarkable mother."

EVEN AS A CHILD he had an unusual interest in public speakers and performers. He was later to recall in connection with his boyhood: "The famous orators were those who could cause jurors to weep. The popular preachers were those who could make the most noise while picturing hell-fire. A really successful funeral could be heard a mile away."

IN HIS SECOND YEAR of high school he failed to respond to the teacher's assignment of a topic for a composition, until she granted his request to select his own topic, "A Basket of Potatoes." It was later published in the local

Gazette. In it he wrote: "Friends, remember this; in the tough, earnest battle of life the big potatoes will go to the top and the small ones will go to the bottom. . . . Whenever you see a small potatoe in the top of the basket, somebody's holding it there."

IN AN unpublished manuscript entitled "Prairie Kings of Yesterday" he described his boyhood recollections and the history of the "land barons" who participated in the pioneer settlement of Newton and surrounding counties, and the abutting counties in Illinois. They were not the usual breed of pioneers who came with little means, a few tools, and large families to carve out a farmstead in the wilderness. They "were masterful and aggressive characters . . . from New York State or New England and brought with them the manners and highly civilized traditions of the East." They came to build new fortunes or to supplement existing ones by acquiring thousands of acres of cheap land upon which to graze imported cattle. They led colorful lives, as evidenced by traditional stories still being told about them not found in the local histories.

Edward C. Sumner and Dr. Orlando Bush were two such entrepreneurs. Sumner was born in Vermont and Bush in Indiana of parents from Berkshire County, Massachusetts. When Dr. Bush was dying, Abigail, Sumner's widow, came to comfort and console him. He responded by saying, "That's mighty kind of you Mrs. Sumner, but this is the end. When I get to the other side, do you know what I'm going to do, first of all? I'm going to hunt up old Ed and tell him that there hasn't been a damned cent made in the cattle business since he died. It'll be a great relief to him."

ADE LIVED IN KENTLAND where he attended school. Of his work on the farm during the summer months in his high school years he said: "I did not volunteer; I was drafted. My parents thought if they kept me away from the gaities and temptations of a village of eight hundred people I might grow up to be a good citizen."

THE LENDING OF BOOKS, never returned, may have been on his mind when he seriously advocated a national holiday to be known as "Returning Day." One would observe this day by "the restoration to proper owners of everything borrowed during the preceding year, with special reference to books, umbrellas and garden implements."

HE WAS WIDELY TRAVELED. To those who might wish to, but could not, he had this message: "It may afford consolation to a large number of people who remain at home to know that only about five per cent of foreign travel is really worth while. . . . You pay for what you get, not in money alone, but in hardships, annoyances, and long periods of dumb, patient waiting."

ADE WAS A VERY KIND PERSON, never wishing to offend even in attempting answers to letters received from eccentric people. He replied to a woman who wrote "urging him to think about saving his soul" in part as follows: "You are wasting a lot of penmanship on someone who does not deserve so much attention. You write a good hand and use good English and you seem to know your Scriptures. . . . I am quite sure that your interest in my behalf is sincere and unselfish and I am duly thankful, even if I am a little amazed and upset to receive a letter nineteen pages long." When she responded with still another letter, he replied: "I am wondering what I can do to cause you to desist in your strenuous efforts in behalf of my spiritual welfare. I have adopted my own way of life and my own tenets of belief and I fear that they cannot be changed even by your eloquent and persistent reasoning. I must request you, as politely as possible, to refrain from these labors in my behalf."

AS TO HIMSELF he wrote: "My enthusiasms include golf, travel, horse-racing, and the spoken drama. My antipathies are social show-offs, bigots on religion, fanatics on total abstinence, and all persons who take themselves seriously."

Dale Fleming

14

Two

MANY PERSONS, now unknown, have unsuspectingly earned a place in history by their influence upon lives of those who later became famous.

Around the year 1880, a teen-age railroad errand boy, wishing to better his position and pay, applied for a job as brakeman. The road superintendent turned to his brawny assistants saying, "Look at this little squirt who wants to be a brakeman." This caustic response would have intimidated one of less ambition, but it only increased the fierce determination of this small, slightly built youth to succeed. The superintendent could not have imagined that Kenesaw Mountain Landis (1866–1944), the rejected applicant, at the age of twenty-seven would be one of a distinguished group leaving Washington D.C. in a special Pullman car bound for the opening of the Columbian Exposition in Chicago in 1893. This party included President and Mrs.

Grover Cleveland, Secretary of the Interior, Hoke Smith, Secretary of the Navy, Hilary A. Herbert, Kenesaw Mountain Landis, the personal secretary of Walter Q. Gresham, the newly appointed Secretary of State, and Thomas F. Bayard, the former Secretary of State. Nor could the superintendent have guessed that this scrawny upstart would in 1905 be appointed by President Theodore Roosevelt as judge of the Federal District Court for Northern Illinois at Chicago, or that he would later become nationally famous as the first Commissioner of Organized Baseball from 1921 until his death in 1944.

*L*ANDIS was not a Hoosier by birth. When he was a small child his father moved the family from Millville, Ohio, where he was born, to Cass County, Indiana. Here he spent his youthful, formative years. He was proud of his rural Indiana background. While occupying the Federal bench in Chicago, he was frequently referred to as "that tough Hoosier judge." When Commissioner he at one time made arrangements to play golf with a group of New York sports writers. When he inquired if they would be ready to tee off at 9 o'clock, one complained of the early hour. Landis fumed, saying, "If you had been brought up on a farm as I was, you would know that 9 o'clock is the middle of the day!"

WITHOUT notifying his parents, he dropped out of high school to take a job in a general store. Here his study of human nature began, listening to "orators and arguers who used to gather around the cracker barrel in an Indiana general store in the early eighties." He later acquired an Isaac Pitman textbook, taught himself shorthand, and in 1883 became the court reporter for the Cass County Circuit Court. Becoming interested in the law, he made up the lack of high school credits at night, completed law courses, and was admitted to the Illinois bar in 1891. He was later to remark, "Because I'm a lawyer, persons naturally think I'm a college graduate. But I'm not, and I'm proud of it. I don't go around shouting that I never went to college; I just keep my mouth shut about where I acquired my knowledge of the law."

THERE WERE conflicting opinions about his conduct as a judge. A New York editor considered him to be "an irascible, short-tempered, tyrannical despot." Others held that he "ran a lively court, badgering witnesses, lawyers and reporters." During one trial he was

18

shocked to hear a defendant frankly admit on the witness stand that he burned important documents in order to conceal evidence. Landis interrupted his testimony to inquire what caused him to do this. The witness replied, "Because I was *noivous*." The judge then asked, "Are you nervous now?" He replied, "I don't know." Landis then charged down from the bench and grabbing the man's hand, "took out his watch and seriously counted the defendant's pulse." He then announced: "No, you don't seem nervous, but you have every reason to be, for in about ten minutes you are going to jail."

AT TIMES he would become impatient with the slow progress in the examining of a witness, believed by reporters to be because he was anxious to get out to Wrigley Field, and "poking a long, menacing finger in the direction of the witness box" would exclaim, "Now let's stop fooling around, and tell exactly what did happen, without reciting your life history."

STILL OTHERS believed him to be "lenient and humane as well as tough and severe." One cold, windy day in Chicago after sentencing a defendant, the judge noted as the man was leaving the courtroom that he had no overcoat. He promptly instructed the baliff, "Fetch my overcoat and give it to this man." The prisoner donned the judge's coat which he wore to the Federal Penitentiary at Leavenworth, Kansas.

LANDIS was greatly amused, and frequently told a story about Donie Bush, a famous short-stop. Bush was summoned to his office to answer charges about his conduct toward umpires. When informed that one in particular claimed his remarks to be "not only profane but also obscene," Bush replied, "That's a darn lie. I never said a profane, obscene thing in my life. All I called him was a blankety-blank-blank!"

IT WAS SAID that Landis "was not a religious man, insofar as creeds, church-going and any outward display of worship were concerned." He apparently was quite the opposite of his Swiss ancestor, a Mennonite, who "was decapitated at Geneva for his religious convictions back in the sixteenth century." Upon his death, Kenesaw left instructions that his body be cremated, that there should be no memorial service. He once remarked that "they always can think of the most wonderful things about a man after he is dead."

AT THE AGE OF EIGHTEEN I came into possession of a packet of letters written by a Civil War soldier to his wife during his service in Company A of the 87th Infantry Regiment, Indiana Volunteers, from Jasper County. The 87th Regiment participated in the important

Atlanta campaign in northwestern Georgia under the Union forces of Maj. Gen. William T. Sherman, including the battle at Kennesaw Mountain in 1864. At that time the only surviving member of this company, George Morgan, was living in Jasper County. On the basis of his vivid recollections and the information supplied by these letters, I embarked upon the ambitious project of writing a narrative story of the Civil War. From this source I learned that Abraham Landis, a surgeon in the Union army, who was wounded in the Battle at Kennesaw Mountain, was the father of Kenesaw Mountain Landis, the then Commissioner of Organized Baseball.

On the morning of October 5, 1935, I sat in the impressive inner office of Commissioner Landis, at 333 North Michigan Avenue, in Chicago, nervously waiting to interview him for the purpose of my story. I was also very curious to meet this controversial figure of the sports world though oblivious of the fact that he was a student of the Civil War. I was also not aware of his explosive disposition. He shortly entered from an adjoining room and quickly related that his father, on June 27, 1864, while attending the wounds of a Union soldier on the mountain side, was himself struck in the leg by a Confederate cannon ball. The leg later had to be amputated. This incident accounted for the name given his son who was born on November 20, 1866. When I attempted to ask him some question, he leaped up from his desk and in a loud, rasping voice exclaimed, "Here you are an author and don't know the War was over in 1865!" He then excused himself and darted back into the adjoining room. Before I had a chance to recover from my embarrassment, he returned, slapping me cordially on the back as he said, "That was Billy Sunday who just came up to see me." The interview ended when he thrust his autographed picture into my hands and quickly disappeared.

LANDIS DIED on November 25, 1944, and "men in high councils of the nation, editors, soldiers, jurists, physicians and scientists" mourned his passing.

24

Three

JOHN ADE (1828–1914), the father of George Ade, noted Hoosier author and playwright, was born in England. He was twelve years of age when his parents emigrated to the United States. As a young man, with a wife and daughter, he migrated from Ohio to the village of Morocco, Indiana, in 1853, becoming one of the early pioneer settlers of Newton County. In 1860 he moved to the town of Kentland, the family home for the ensuing fifty-four years. He was a blacksmith, storekeeper, public official and banker. At the age of eighty-three he wrote a book entitled, Newton County, published in 1911, now a collector's item, which the author described as, "A Collection of Historical Facts and Personal Recollections Concerning Newton County, Indiana, From 1853 to 1911." The book is interesting, aside from its historical value, for several reasons.

In an unpublished manuscript written by George Ade, entitled, "Prairie Kings of Yesterday" he quotes from this book by saying that "the primitive nature of our neighborhood is well described in a book written by my father," but otherwise making no comments as to its contents, the name or the year it was written. In the biography of George Ade written by Fred C. Kelly, the author makes no mention of his father's book. If George Ade did not have a considerable part in the writing and publication of this book, as some believe, one is unable to read it without concluding that George Ade acquired some of his love of the English language and his ability as an author and story-teller from his father.

WHILE JOHN ADE "was a pillar of the Campbellite or Christian Church . . . and sometimes preached" he includes a chapter in his book entitled, "Ingersoll's Tribute." This was an address by Robert G. Ingersoll at Indianapolis on September 20, 1876, which he included as a "fitting conclusion to the record of our patriotic soldiers" of the Civil War. A portion of this address reads as follows:

"The past rises before me like a dream . . .

we see all the dead whose dust we have covered with flowers. . . . They sleep in the land they made free, under the flag they rendered stainless, under the solemn pines, the sad hemlocks, the tearful willows and the embracing vines. They sleep beneath the shadows of the clouds, careless alike of the sunshine or the storm, each in the windowless palace of rest."

IN ANOTHER CHAPTER entitled, "A Few Stories" he relates one of his own experiences, as follows:

"One little incident will illustrate the condition of the minds of some people regarding superstitions a little over fifty years ago. One day, while working in the old log blacksmith shop in Morocco, a man came in with a little job of work. While waiting for it to be finished he related to me his troubles. It seemed from his story that some time before he, or some of his family, had been having a little falling out with an old lady in their neighborhood, and from that time they were unable to make their butter 'come' although they had spent much time and put forth a lot of hard labor at the churn. Being unable to account for this condition of things on any reasonable grounds, they finally came to the conclusion that the old woman with whom they had been quarreling had 'bewitched' the cow. The more they thought of it the stronger became the conviction. After telling of his troubles he wanted my advice as to how this 'spell' might be removed. My experience along the line of witchcraft having been limited, I had to draw on my imagination somewhat. My first thought was to recommend the black cat cure. That was to take a black cat and cut off three inches of its tail, one inch at a time. Upon reflection I concluded that would be pretty rough on the cat, so I abandoned that treatment. I then told him to go home and fill his churn one-third full of water, take the kingbolt out of his wagon, put one end in the fire, and, when it got quite hot, to swing it three times around his head, shout as loudly as he could, and then stick the hot end of the kingbolt into the water in the churn. That, I told him, I thought was the best thing to do under the circumstances.

"He went home and I had almost forgotten the circumstances, when one day a few weeks afterwards he again came to the shop. This brought the whole matter fresh to mind, and I asked him if he had done as directed.

"He answered that he had done so and that since doing it there had been no trouble with the butter proposition. To make the remedy still more certain of having produced these results, he said: 'And I want to tell you, right at that very time that I done it, that old woman who had bewitched the cow had a spell of sickness.'

"Which proved positively that she had bewitched the cow and also demonstrated the efficacy of the remedy. It also proved that my misplaced sympathy for the black cat had resulted in misfortune for the old lady, although I had not meant to do her any harm."

30

Four

JAMES WHITCOMB RILEY (1849–1916), was born in the town of Greenfield, Indiana. He became, and is today, the most widely known Hoosier poet, principally remembered for such poems as, When The Frost Is on the Punkin, The Old Swimmin' Hole, Little Orphant Annie, The Raggedy Man, *and* Out to Old Aunt Mary's.

Riley had many sides, not now generally known. As a slender, blue-eyed youth of sixteen he left school to become a sign painter, amateur musician, poet, newspaper editor, lecturer, aspiring actor, mimic and story-teller. Having little interest in the classical forms of verse, he developed his own homespun style described by Hamlin Garland as "a humble crop gathered from the corners of rail fences, from vines which clamber upon the porches of small villages, and from the weedy side-walks of quiet towns far from the great markets of the world."

He was not the simple rustic reflected by many of his poems, was not socially inclined, and in his later years appeared as "urbanity itself, with polished good taste, meticulously groomed, dignified, with gold-headed walking stick and white carnation boutonniere."

*O*N APRIL 16, 1885, two years after publication of the first book of poems including, *The Old Swimmin' Hole,* Riley wrote a letter in response to an inquiry about his life, reading in part as follows:

"I am lying flat o' my gifted back and writing with my toes. I have seen better days. . . . I wrote to Mr. McIntyre and McConnell yesterday, but concealed my real condition, knowing both would encourage me to die—one wanting to *funeralize* and the other to *obituarize.* You ask for my life, but I'd rather give you my money. I was thirty-one years old last spring. Five feet six in height . . . I am a blonde of fair complexion, with an almost ungovernable trend for brunettes. . . . Used to make a lot of money but never had any on hand. It all evaporated in some mysterious way. My standard weight is a hundred and thirty-five. . . . My father is a lawyer and lured me into his office once for a three-month sentence. But I made good my escape, and under cover of the kindly night, I fled up the Pike with a patent-medicine concert-wagon, and had a good time for two or three of the happiest years of my life. Next I struck a country paper and tried to edit, but the proprietor he wanted to do that, and wouldn't let me, and in about a year I quit tryin' and let him have his own way, and now it's the hardest thing in the world for me to acknowledge that he is still an editor and a most successful one. Later I went back to Greenfield and engaged in almost anything but work and so became quite prominent. Noted factions and public houses began to regard me attentively, and no grand jury was complete without my presence! I wasn't however, considered wholly lost till I began to publish poetry brazenly affixing my own name to it. But I couldn't get any money for it, although stranger editors wrote me letters of praise regarding it. Then I sent a little of the best of it to two or three real poets East, and they commended it, and I showed their letters, and have been paid ever since. Still I am not rich. A skating-rink proprietor who yearns to be a poet should be regarded with suspicion. . ."

GEORGE ADE, author, playwright and world traveler, was a friend of presidents and many other famous people of his day. Yet in the later years of his life when asked by James Kelley, his biographer, as to whom among the various celebrities he had known "was the most interesting." He replied: "The most unusual, the most amusing, the most interesting beyond all comparisons was James Whitcomb Riley. He was the most lovable, the most altogether different person I ever knew." Though following this statement, Ade "talked about Riley for a long time," Kelley failed to elaborate further other than recording his praise of Riley as a story-teller.

RILEY was a frequent guest of George Ade's at Hazelden, and because he liked to sit

under a certain oak tree it became known as
the "Riley tree." It is obvious that as a result of
these visits Ade was later to say: "He was the
best story-teller I ever heard because his character impersonations were vivid and accurate
and convincing beyond all belief." He also said
that a lot of his stories "were pointless unless

the listeners happened to be those who love the right kind of nonsense. And I don't think Riley ever told these stories unless he knew all about the listeners." This probably accounts for the fact that unfortunately few were preserved. One that Ade and others considered to be the best was the trombone story.

Wesley Hanchfield, a young man from Greenfield, played "the second alto in the town band." At a performance in Indianapolis "he saw and heard, for the first time, a slide-trombone." Thereafter his great ambition was to own this instrument which he later acquired. He then had a tinner contrive a case for it that was "very unusual in appearance." Wesley came to Riley, then a sign painter, and had his name printed on the side of the case. However after this was done, to avoid having "to answer so many fool questions" about what was in the case he had the name of the instrument added. Finally he was still not satisfied until the name of the state was added. The story ends with the explanation that thereafter "Mr. Hanchfield attracted considerable attention whenever he turned out with the band boys, carrying a metallic box of weird design, on which was painted:

WESLEY HANCHFIELD

TROMBONE

Indiana"

RILEY was a very private person and "shrank from idle and promiscuous friendships." One morning he walked from his house to the store of the Bobbs-Merrill Company in downtown Indianapolis. "As he came to the first corner the policeman saluted him and said: 'This is a fine morning Mr. Riley.' Riley did not contradict him." He was a familiar figure and by the time he reached the office of Will Bobbs "fifty people informed him that the weather was beautiful." Mr. Bobbs greeted him, saying, "Well, this is a lovely morning." Unable to restrain himself any longer, Riley "shouted, so loud you could hear him all over the store: 'It must be! Everybody speaks very highly of it.' "

"EVERY MORNING when I wake up the first thought that comes to me is: This is the day they get on to me."

RILEY'S FATHER was ambitious for his son to become a lawyer like himself, and to please his father "he struggled to satisfy his wishes" for a short time. The law was not to his liking, and legal proceedings were to him "dense with stupidity." He was later to repeat the charge of a rural justice of the peace to a jury: "Gentlemen, if you believe what the counsel for the plaintiff says, you will find for the plaintiff. If you believe what the counsel for the defendant says, you will find for the defendant. But if, like me, you believe neither the counsel for the plaintiff nor the counsel for the defendant, the Lord only knows what you will find."

THOUGH HE KEPT his letters and personal papers in strict order, he frequently was distressed about his inability to locate some item he had so carefully filed away. At such time he was known to say, "A place for everything and everything *someplace* else."

IT WAS BELIEVED that some of Riley's stories of people and situations were entirely of his own creation. One was an experience he was supposed to have had with Bill Nye, a noted humorist of that day. They were waiting at a small railway station to catch a train for Birmingham where they were to perform. Riley had not shaved that morning and inquired of the station agent about a barber. He explained there was none in the village but that there was an old colored gentleman down the road who did so on occasion. He was sent for and the result is as related by George Ade:

"In a little while an old colored fellow with a long board under his arm and carrying a rusty valise appeared at the station. He said that he was the barber. Riley said he wanted a shave.

The barber laid his board lengthwise on the bench in the waiting-room and said to Mr. Riley, 'Lay down.'

"Mr. Riley wanted to know why he couldn't be shaved while sitting up and the barber replied, 'I can't do it 'less you lay down. You'll be the fust live one I have eveh shaved.' "

WHEN A PRINTER friend, who had obviously in the past set the type for some of Riley's newspaper contributions, married a Greenfield girl, he wrote the following letter to the local paper: "We know little of the bride other than that she is fair and womanly beyond all words; but as for the compositor—we know him and recall with emotions of awe the way he used to tangle up our silken sentences and crush and mangle beyond all hope of recognition the many prattling puns we intrusted to his care. The manifold inflictions he heaped upon us then we bore in mute despair; now we exult, for he is wedded to another. . ."

RILEY LIVED in a world apart from the general daily concerns and activities of the people around him, and from which he found the stimulus for what he believed to be his mission in life. While he had no interest in politics he did attend at least one meeting which may have changed the course of his life. A national campaign in October, 1876, brought Robert G. Ingersoll to Greenfield, who spoke in part as follows: "Nothing is more marvelous than the common everyday facts of everyday life. The age of wonders is not in the past. There are millions of miracles under our feet. In the lives of the people, here and now, are all the comedy and tragedy they can comprehend." Riley "listened for two hours to eloquence that remained golden in memory for forty years."

HIS PUBLISHED POEMS, numbering more than one thousand, are written in a so-called Hoosier dialect that some contend "was his own invention." His rare attempts at prose writing are not only miniature portraits of his own life and thoughts, but indicate his exceptional descriptive powers. Examples are found in a short story entitled, "Tale Of A Spider."

"I want it distinctly understood that I am superstitious, notwithstanding the best half of my life, up to the very present, has been spent in the emphatic denial of that fact. And I am painfully aware that this assertion at so late a date can but place my former character in a most unenviable light; yet for reasons you will never know I have, with all due deliberation, determined to hold the truth up stark and naked, to the world, with the just acknowledgement, shorn of all attempts at palliation or excuse, that for the best half of my life I have been simply a coward and a liar. . . .

"The silence of the night without was deep. Not a footstep in the street below, and not a sound of any living earthly thing fell on the hearing, though that sense was whetted to such acuteness I could plainly hear the ticking of a clock somewhere across the street.

"All things about the room were in usual order. My letters on the desk were folded as I answered them, and filed away; my books were arranged in order, and my manuscripts tucked out of sight and mind, and no scrap of paper to remind me of my never-ended work, save the blank sheet that always lies in readiness for me to pounce upon with any vagrant thought that comes along, and close beside it the open inkstand and the idle pen."

RILEY WAS KNOWN for keeping irregular hours, sometimes working very late at night if seized by an inspiration to write. However story has it that one day he met a friend who said to him: "Mr. Riley, you don't look very well. You look as though you had been losing sleep." Riley quickly replied: "I've just been through a terrible experience. I was up all night—having a poem!"

IN THE DECEMBER 1927 issue of the Cosmopolitan magazine, an article appears entitled, "The Stories That Riley Used To Tell" written by George Ade and illustrated by John T. McCutcheon. One of the stories had to do with Riley's dislike when on a lecture tour of the reception committees "putting him on exhibition." Ade describes the following incident:

Once he came to Lafayette and one of the local celebrities, a distinguished Colonel who was keenly interested in the early history of Tippecanoe County, grabbed Riley and took him up to the famous "Battle Ground," where General William Henry Harrison fought his decisive battle with the Indians in 1811.

The state had lately parked the whole battlefield which is a wooded hilltop overlooking the valley of the Wabash River. One of the improvements had been an ornate iron fence enclosing the whole park.

The Colonel walked Mr. Riley over the hilltop, explaining every detail of the battle.

When he had finished his two-hour recital he and Mr. Riley were at the lower end of the battlefield and Mr. Riley was leaning wearily against the expensive iron fence donated by the State of Indiana.

"Now, Mr. Riley," asked the Colonel, "have I told you everything you want to know? Is it all clear to you?"

"There's only one thing I don't quite understand," said Riley.

"What's that?"

"I don't understand how the Indians ever got over this fence."

It was a six-mile ride from Battle Ground to Lafayette and a long ride in a buggy, but they say the Colonel didn't speak to the children's poet—not once—all the way in.

Five

JAMES E. WATSON (1863–1948), was born at Winchester, Indiana. He was a member of the U.S. Congress for twenty-nine years, first elected to the House of Representatives in 1894, and later serving in the Senate from 1916 to 1933. He served under Presidents Cleveland, McKinley, Roosevelt, Taft, Wilson, Harding, Coolidge and Hoover. He also knew Presidents Harrison, Grant, Hayes and Arthur.

His memoirs entitled, As I Knew Them, published in 1936, he described as being "devoted very largely to my personal experiences in politics." Any interest in his accounts, as party leader, of the internal political struggles and legislative enactments during the period of his service in the Congress is now largely confined to the student or political historian.

Senator Watson possessed a delightful sense of humor, and of far greater importance and

47

interest now is in that portion of his book relating to the little known stories about presidents, famous members of Congress and those not so famous, which is the source of the following.

IN HIS FIRST campaign speech for Congress at the village of Andersonville, he orated for two hours. Afterwards as he drove home by buggy, accompanied by Jack Ross, a country lawyer and chairman of the meeting, he waited anxiously for some comment on his speech. When none came and he pressed for an opinion, the chairman's only response was, "Well, you did pretty good." Not satisfied, he finally inquired if he had missed anything, to which Ross replied, "Yes, you missed two damned good places to quit!"

"IN THOSE DAYS in both the Senate and House, particularly the Senate, it was considered grossly out of place for a new man to make a speech. Following this custom, I put in my first term looking around, observing, becoming acquainted with the other members, and informing myself on the methods of legislation. . . . Senator Joe Brown of Georgia, expressed it by saying that the first couple of months he was a senator he looked around with awe on the assembled senators and wondered how in the world he had ever happened to land in such company. After that, for the next three months, he looked around at them and wondered how the other fellows ever got into the Senate. And after that they all looked around at one another and wondered how on earth they were all going to stay in the Senate."

ONE DAY a "pompous, bombastic" member of the House from Illinois concluded a long speech on the floor with the statement: "Like the great Commoner from Kentucky, Henry Clay, I would rather be right than be president." Thomas B. Reed, the brilliant and witty Speaker of the House who was standing close to him added so that the entire House could easily hear: "The gentleman from Illinois need not be alarmed. He will never be either."

AT ONE TIME newspaper correspondents were interviewing Thomas B. Reed, Speaker of the House, as to why it was that financial experts, comprising the Committee on Banking and Currency, could never seem to agree when considering pending financial legislation. Reed's explanation was that "there is something about the intimate study of finance that, if a man continues it long enough, disqualifies him from talking intelligently upon any other subject, and, if he continues it still longer, disqualifies him from talking intelligently upon that."

HIS PARTY POSITION of leadership afforded him close contact with the occupants of the White House, which made possible his description of President Theodore Roosevelt.

"He was eternally at something or other. He never wasted a moment. . . . He had on his desk poetry, philosophy, fiction, works on metaphysics, psychology, zoology, and so on, and if he had ten minutes of unoccupied time, he grabbed one of these books and plunged at once into its pages. He had the power of concentration developed to a high degree, and he could go from one subject to another, or one book to another with complete control. . . . One morning I went over to the White House at eight-thirty. He was just starting out for a walk and asked me to accompany him. When I walk, I take a long swinging stride, while the President walked with short choppy steps. I got weary in a little while, but of course I had to keep pace with the administration and trudged along until I was pretty well worn out. To add to my discomfort, our course led through Rock Creek Park, and when we came to the stream, instead of deviating and seeking a bridge, Roosevelt strode right through the water which was well up to the tops of his shoes, with never a break in his flow of speech, and just as if this was the most natural thing in the world to do. I perforce accompanied him and soon found myself quite uncomfortable as a result."

51

"CONSIDER in swift review a few of our greatest orators: Patrick Henry, Henry Clay, Daniel Webster, John C. Calhoun, Charles Sumner, James G. Blaine, William Jennings Bryan, Albert J. Beveridge—not one of these ever became president. While it is true that many of our presidents have not been notable speakers, it is not true that they were distinguished for their oratorical power alone, and in the last analysis one cannot help feeling that the people want men who act rather than men who orate, and men of abiding stability as compared with those they evidently believe have a more fleeting conception of things however meteoric they may appear at the moment. When the fiery comet comes and fills the heavens, everybody rushes out to see it every night it can be viewed, but after it has disappeared, they turn hopefully to the old North Star still shining serene and undisturbed."

PRESIDENT William Howard Taft was a very large man with a "big frontal development." At a time when Taft's fondness for Theodore Roosevelt had commenced to cool, Senator Watson was conferring with the president in his private office when Senator Chauncey DePew of New York, a noted lawyer and orator and story-teller, entered the room. Shortly thereafter as he was preparing to depart, and much to the amazement of Watson, DePew patted Taft on the stomach, saying, "What are you going to name it when it comes, Mr. President?" Taft quickly responded: "Well, if it is a boy, I'll call it William; if it is a girl, I'll call it Theodora; but if it turns out to be just wind, I'll call it Chauncey."

"SOME WAG started the saying years ago, and it has been added to many times since, that the character of each president could be told by the manner in which he handled his callers and the method by which he disposed of his visitors. And it was said that Grant, the great soldier, drilled them out; that Hayes, the first extreme temperance president, dried them out; that

Garfield preached them out; that Arthur smiled and bowed them out; that Cleveland, in his first term nudged and elbowed them out; that Harrison froze them out; that McKinley loved them out; that Roosevelt rode them out; that Taft laughed them out; that Wilson shut them out altogether; that Harding joked them out; that Coolidge let them talk themselves out and that Hoover just went out with them."

"OF COURSE I regard lack of humor as a misfortune in any person. When a man cannot see the humorous phases of human life or take advantage of them either in private conversation or public speech to impress some point of his own, well, in my judgment, he is most unfortunately constituted."

"NEWS that has about it the tincture of sensation will be used by the public press, while plain statements of argument go by the boards."

JOSEPH GURNEY CANNON (1836–1926), at one time "known familiarly and fondly to millions as Uncle Joe, was one of the most picturesque and controversial members of the House of Representatives, and without doubt the most iron-handed Speaker of the House. He was a member of the House from Danville, Illinois, for forty-six years and a close friend of Senator Watson for more than thirty years. Watson states that "though he was apparently rough and tumble and uncouth he was inwardly as gentle as a child." He was loved by his many friends in and out of Congress and greatly feared by his enemies. When Mark Twain came to Washington he always called on Uncle Joe. The stories told by him and about him are legendary. He was particularly criticized for his coarse speech. His only known response to the charge of profanity was recorded by Senator Watson upon the occasion of attending a political rally in his behalf at Danville. The story as told by Watson relates to a "preacher in the town, I will call him Jones, who was noted for his beautiful literary and scholastic sermons, which were really lectures, but who was generally supposed to be slightly short on piety." At the close of a reception held in honor of Uncle Joe, he inquired of one of his supporters as to what he might do to enhance his election. The constituent criticized his profanity, saying that "there are mutterings about sending a man who is so outlandishly profane to represent their district."

Uncle Joe replied: "Well, I guess these folks are right about my cussin,' but they must remember that I belong to a different age. I was born at a time when about everybody swore and about everybody drank liquor and even preachers had it on their sideboards. I suppose that, boylike, when I started swearin' I thought it was smart and kept it up for that reason; but now it has become a fixed habit with me as to be an ineradicable part of my nature, and in private conversation I can't even emphasize if I don't put in a few cuss words to show my real feeling. Everybody who knows me knows that I would not call on our common Maker to damn any of his creatures. Oh, I'm with my cussin' a good deal like Brother Jones is with his prayin', don't mean a damned thing by it."

WHILE CALVIN COOLIDGE had an occasional drink when governor of Massachusetts, as president, "he religiously abstained from the use of all intoxicants, and, of course would not suffer their presence in the White House." There are many stories still told reflecting his droll sense of humor. One that is less known is a story told to Senator Watson, which he believed to be true, about Coolidge when governor.

A visitor we shall identify as Mr. Brown called on Coolidge. After they had talked for a while, his secretary said to him: "Governor, perhaps Mr. Brown would like a little drink." Collidge produced a key, unlocked a trunk from which he took a bottle of whiskey, and poured out a small portion in a glass for his guest. He then replaced the bottle in the trunk and locked it. In a short time another visitor joined the conference which we will identify as Mr. Smith. In a short time thereafter the secretary said to the governor: "Perhaps Mr. Smith would like a little drink." Again the governor took out his key, unlocked the trunk, and pouring out a very small amount of whiskey in the bottom of the glass, handed it to the guest. He then replaced the bottle in the trunk and locked it. Mr. Smith downed the drink in one swallow. The secretary then said to the governor: "Perhaps Mr. Brown would like another drink," to which Coolidge replied: "No he's had his."

DURING the Coolidge administration the House passed a measure increasing the salaries of the members of Congress. It was afterwards approved by the Senate on the day that William E. Borah, the Senator from Idaho, was absent. Upon his return to the Senate the following day, Borah made a speech denouncing the actions of the Senate. In reply, Senator Thomas Heflin of Alabama made one of the wittiest speeches "ever heard up in either House." At the conclusion Senator Borah did not respond, something that "rarely happened in his long and prominent career."

The following are the remarks of Senator Heflin:

"If the Senator from Idaho does not want to take his salary, oh, Mr. President, he can refuse it; but I believe that when it comes due we can induce him to take it. He will be like Private John Allen was.

"John Allen went home from New Orleans once after he had been down there fishing with the boys. They had treated him royally, wined and dined him, until he was a little weary and worn, and when he arrived home he saw his doctor at the station. He said: 'My wife is a crank on the prohibition question. I haven't got a drop in my grip. I feel that I must have a little to taper off on. Won't you send a bottle up and beg her yourself to give it to me as medicine?'

"The doctor agreed that he would.

"When John arrived at home, his wife met him and said: 'How are you feeling, my dear?'

"He said: 'Very poorly. I have never felt quite so weak. I feel like I need a stimulant, but I am not going to take it. I will never touch another drop of it; never, never.'

" 'Well, now, John, you must not be cranky on the subject,' she said.

"He said, 'No, I have made up my mind.'

"He lay down on the bed, and the phone rang. It was the doctor. 'Mrs. Allen, I am sending up a quart. You make a nice mint julep and force your husband to drink it. I saw him at the station. He is weak and worn to a frazzle. You give him this mint julep.'

"The brilliant John Allen was lying there on the bed, and he heard the ice chunks clinking in the glass. His wife bore the mint julep into his bedroom in graceful, queenly fashion, with frost on the sides of the glass, a bank of sugar at the bottom, and three strawberries nestling thereon like so many eggs in a bird's nest, while the mint leaned over the rim of the glass.

"His wife took it up to the bedside and said: 'Now, I want you to take this.'

"He said: 'I can't do it. I have said I will not do it.'

"She said: 'But John, you must drink it. The doctor says for you to take it. The doctor has prescribed it, you must take it.'

"He said: 'I can't, and I won't.'

" 'Won't you take it for me?' she pleaded.

"He said: 'If you put it that way, I will.'

"He took that mint julep glass in his hand. The amber-colored liquid flowed over the velvet folds of his stomach like a dewdrop sinking into the heart of a rose.

"So Private Allen disposed of the contents of the glass and looking up at his wife said: 'I believe I'm going to sleep now, but before I fall into a deep, sweet sleep, let me ask you a question. When did the doctor tell you to give me another mint julep?'

"She said: 'In two hours.'

" 'Well,' he said, 'if I am asleep wake me, and if I won't take it, make me. . .' "

Six

LEWIS (LEW) WALLACE (1827–1905), was born at Brookville, Indiana. One could best briefly characterize his life by borrowing from Shakespeare's famous lines, "all the world's a stage, and one man in his lifetime plays many parts." He was a lawyer, soldier, author, poet, painter, musician and craftsman. As a soldier he participated in the Mexican War (1846–47), and rose to the rank of major in the Civil War, and later was a member of the court that tried the persons charged with the conspiracy in the assassination of President Lincoln. He was Governor of the New Mexico Territory in 1878, and minister to Turkey in 1881.

However he is best known as the author of three romantic historical novels, The Fair God, Ben Hur, and The Prince of India. While described as "an incurable romantic" and that "his novels are the setting down of his fantasies," he demonstrated his great descriptive powers in a *little known contribution to the historic lore of one of the giants of American history, contained in his biography published after his death in 1906. From 1849 to 1853 he maintained a law office in Covington, Indiana. One day he and his fellow barrister, Daniel W. Voorhees, hired a horse and buggy and drove across the state line to Danville, Illinois, to attend a court session on the following day. This in his own words is the experience he relates:*

"WE REACHED THE TOWN about dusk and stopped at the tavern. The bar-room, when we entered it after supper, was all a-squeeze with residents, spiced with parties to suits pending, witnesses and jurors. The ceiling was low, and we had time to admire the depth and richness of the universal smoke-stain of the wooden walls. To edge in we had to bide our time. Every little while there would be bursts of laughter, and now and then a yell of delight. At last, within the zone of sight, this was what we saw. In front of us a spacious pioneer fireplace all aglow with a fire scientifically built. On the right of the fireplace sat three of the best story-tellers of Indiana, Edward A. Hannegan, Dan Mace, and John Pettit. Opposite them, a broad brick hearth intervening, were two.strangers to me whom inquiry presently identified as famous lawyers and yarn-spinners of Illinois.

"One may travel now from the Kennebec to Puget Sound and never see such a tournament as the five men were holding; only instead of splintering lances they were swapping anecdotes. As to the kind and color of the jokes submitted to the audience, while not always chaste, they never failed to hit home.

"The criss-crossing went on till midnight, and for a long time it might not be said whether Illinois or Indiana was ahead. There was one of the contestants, however, who arrested my attention early, partly by his stories, partly by his appearance. Out of the mist of years he comes to me now exactly as he appeared then. His hair was thick, course, and defiant; it stood out in every direction. His features were massive, nose long, eyebrows protrusive, mouth large, cheeks hollow, eyes gray and always responsive to humor. He smiled all the time, but never once did he laugh outright. His hands were large, his arms slender and disproportionately long. His legs were a wonder, particularly when he was in narration; he kept crossing and uncrossing them; sometimes it actually seemed he was trying to tie them into a bow-knot. His dress was more than plain; no part of it to fit him. His shirt collar had come from the home laundry innocent of starch. The black cravat about his neck persisted in an ungovernable affinity with his left ear. Altogether I thought him the gauntest, quaintest, and most positively ugly man who had ever attracted me enough to call for study. Still, when he was in speech, my eyes did not quit his face. He held me in unconsciousness. About midnight his competitors were disposed to give in; either their stories were exhausted, or they were tacitly conceding him the crown. From answering them story for story, he gave two or three to their one. At last he took the floor and held it. And looking back, I am now convinced that he frequently invented his replications; which is saying he possessed a marvelous gift of improvisation. Such was *Abraham Lincoln*. And to be perfectly candid, had one stood at my elbow that night in the old tavern and whispered: 'Look at him closely. He will one day be president and the savior of his country,' I had laughed at the idea but a little less heartily than I laughed at the man. Afterwards I came to know him better, and then I did not laugh."

Seven

JACOB PIATT DUNN (1855–1924), was born at
Lawrenceburg, Indiana. He attended the University of Michigan and graduated from Earlham
College in 1874. He became the Indiana State
Librarian in 1891, "and during this service wrote
regularly for the Indianapolis Sentinel. He was
also an editorial writer for the Indianapolis
Star." Between 1888 and 1921, he wrote numerous books relating to the early history of Indiana, the most extensive being five volumes
published in 1919 entitled, Indiana and Indianans, a History of Aboriginal and Territorial Indiana and the Century of Statehood, from which
the following references are taken.

*T*HERE ARE many theories about the origin of the name "Hoosier," the most prominent of which is believed to be derived from the pioneer responding to a knock on the log-cabin door. William E. Wilson, author of *Indiana A History* states: "Others trace the word to a company of hussers who once made a nuisance of themselves in Kentucky by their hard drinking and rowdyism with the result that the term 'hussar' or 'hoosier' was applied to any objectionable outsider in Kentucky, especially the frontiersmen of Indiana from across the river."

Jacob Piatt Dunn devotes an entire chapter to the conflicting origins of the name which includes the following:

"To these theories of the origin of the word may be added one communicated to me by James Whitcomb Riley, whose acquaintance with dialect makes him an authority on the subject. It is evidently of later origin than the others, and not so well known to the public. A casual conversation happening to turn to this subject, he said: 'These stories commonly told about the origin of the word 'Hoosier' are all nonsense. The real origin is found in the pugnacious habits of the early settlers. They were very vicious fighters, and not only gouged and scratched, but frequently bit off noses and ears. This was so ordinary an affair that a settler coming into a bar-room on a morning after a fight, and seeing an ear on the floor would merely push it aside with his foot and carelessly ask, 'Who's ear'? I feel safe in venturing the opinion that this theory is quite as plausible, and almost as well sustained by historical evidence, as any of the others"

IN VOLUME II of *Indiana and Indianans,* the author described the powerful oratorical ability and great descriptive powers of the circuit riding preacher in pioneer times, with illustrations where "the responses of the audience were not always religious in character, although they showed the interest awakened by the discourse."

In one instance "a frontier preacher was holding a meeting in a bar-room—a quite common occurrence—and preaching from the text, 'Seek first the kingdom of God and his righteousness, and all these things shall be added unto you.' He then endeavored, in plain words, to show them the absurdity and folly of serving the devil, saying: 'He is the most wretched being in all the universe; and as misery loves company, he will drag you down to his own fiery abode. If you are seeking for honor, the devil has none to bestow; he is the most dishonorable being that lives. And if you are seeking for wealth, the devil has none of it; if you are to sweep hell from one end to other, you would not get a six-pence.' A large, honest but coarse-looking fellow, sitting right before the preacher, with eyes and mouth wide open, exclaimed, unconsciously: 'God! money is as scarce there as it is here!' "

"IT MUST BE that the isolation of the frontier had a material effect on the religious sentiment of the pioneers. Few men who think do not realize that they are not living as good lives as they might. They may not indulge in crimes or even vices, but they are seldom exercising their virtues to their full capacity. In the early period everybody believed in the Bible. Even professed atheists had a deep-down belief, such as Stevenson pictures in his pirates in *Treasure Island*. They have a story in Owen County of an old farmer who was 'a little near,' who had a son, Absolom, who never got along financially. Absolom finally went to Texas, with his wife and children, to enter some land; and in due time wrote to his father for assistance, stating that he was out of money, could get no work, and his family were suffering from hunger. The old gentleman had a couple of notes that Absolom had given him for borrowed money, and he canceled these, put them in an envelope, and sent them to Absolom. Some time after, his brother-in-law was telling this to James Phillips, a professed infidel of the neighborhood, who indignantly asked, 'Did the old man do that?' 'Yes, he did, and I sent Absolom some money myself.' 'Well, the old scoundrel; he ought to be in hell.' 'But I thought you didn't believe in hell.' 'I didn't; but by God I never saw the necessity for it before.' "

"MOST of the pioneer women had large families and little of the infant mortality was due to stomach trouble. . . . It was not a matter of choice, but of finding material from which a pie could be made, and when all the fruits and berries had been exhausted, as well as pumpkin, squash, sweet-potato and Irish potato, she moved on to vinegar pie. So, in the lack of spices, she utilized lemon and orange peel. So she made preserves of tomatoes and watermelon rinds, and pickled various vegetables. . . . Who that has eaten hotel strawberry shortcake, has not yearned for the kind 'that Mother used to make?' And her 'preventive medicines' were not confined to foods. She made decoctions of medicinal plants, salves, washes, planters and poultices. She not only made soap, but made the lye to make the soap; and this was continued long after 'store soap' was available. Says George W. Sloan: "There was not a large sale for bar soap because all the old women made soft soap. No coal was burned then and there were plenty of wood ashes. The woman saved the ashes, leached them, boiled the lye down until it would float an egg, added her savings of grease to it and made soap. She had learned to add salt, and that made hard soap.' If there is anything in heredity, the average American can look for ingenuity on the maternal as well as the paternal side. And there were dozens of forms of industry in which both sexes participated, such as preserving meats, making candles and grease lamps, making and using dyes, tanning skins, cleaning feathers, and other efforts to add to the comforts, or earn an honest dollar."

IN *Indiana and Indianans,* the author compiled three volumes devoted to detailed histories of Indiana families. In one related to the Andrew family of LaPorte, Indiana, he included a long poem written by Sarah Andrew Shafer, the author of *Day Before Yesterday,* and a granddaughter of James Andrew, reading in part as follows:

"Was it always Spring in the long ago
    At Grandfather's?
Was the orchard hid always by rosy snow?
In the long grass did violets always grow,
While blackbirds paced, their necks aglow,
Under the pines—where softest winds
Rocked the cradle of baby bird
To tunes the sweetest ever heard?
Tunes that come to my longing ears
Over the silence of many years,
Was it always Summer, there, of old,
    At Grandfather's?
Were the wheat fields ever a sea of gold?
Were meadows but carpets gay, unrolled
For the frolic winds to toss and fold?
. . ."

76

Eight

JOHN T. McCUTCHEON (1870–1949), was born in a farmhouse "on a gentle hilltop on the Romney Road a few miles south of Lafayette, Indiana." His colorful career as a reporter, world-traveler, foreign correspondent, illustrator and political cartoonist began shortly after his graduation from Purdue University when "he came to Chicago in the late summer of 1889, with $17 in my pocket and not a friend in the city." He was first employed by the old Chicago Record and Chicago Record-Herald as a newspaper correspondent and illustrator. In 1903 he joined the staff of the Chicago Tribune where he continued to be employed for more than forty years.

The following examples of his wit and art are taken from miscellaneous sources and his book Drawn From Memory, published in 1950.

"*T*HE STORY GOES that soon after my birth, my uncle George sought to console my mother: 'Now don't mind what they say, Clara. He'll look all right after a while.' "

"I SUPPOSE I was much like any other small boy growing up on a farm, unless down there in Indiana we wore more freckles and less shoes. Dressing in our little bare cold room was not a hardship, because we knew nothing different."

"THERE WERE NOT MANY amusements in those days, and such as there were—cornhuskings, barn-raisings, spelling bees, weddings and funerals—were carried on slightly beyond my range of personal recollections. All the children for miles around attended their first theatrical performance when a traveling troupe came to Romney and gave 'Ten Nights in a Barroom.' The show was likewise attended by a lively measles germ, and the ensuing epidemic was exhaustive. What happened in a barroom became of minor importance compared to what happened at home. I had to lie in bed with nothing to do except listen to the killdeers calling across the misty bottom lands down by the creek."

"OUR PARENTS often took us with them when they drove to Lafayette in the surrey. . . . Sometimes my father would stop the horses, get out and be gone for a few mysterious moments. Upon his return our eager voices arose, clamorous for information. 'What's the matter, Pa? What d'you get out for, Pa? Whered you go Pa?' This rapid-fire quiz always brought the same answer. 'Thought I saw a prairie chicken.' Further cross-examination always disclosed his failure to catch the prairie chicken. Often in later years I found this a handy euphemism, with enthusiastic co-operation on the part of my own small sons."

IN 1876, his father, John Barr McCutcheon, "was forced to abandon his life as a drover" and became associated with Purdue University as manager of the commissariat.

In recalling this early period of his life he wrote: "I remember only two things about those days. One was the tremendous excitement when the first electric light was shown in front of the chemical laboratory. The other was the sound of the Chauncey School Bell which summoned me to my first school. It filled me with a sickish foreboding. I hated the school with an intensity that was devastating. Today when I hear a bell of the same flat metallic tone, regardless of my surroundings the same old 'gone' feeling sweeps over me. . . . Many people have sung the power of sounds and smells, the power of fragrances, or certain music, to turn the memory back from now to then. I know many such, not all with such gloomy association as the Chauncey School Bell."

"A FEW YEARS AGO revisited the old farm. Our house had been painted and much beporched, though the front gable was graced by the same rounded triple window. The trees were big and spreading; I could not recognize the one that had been struck by lightning as I sat in my mother's lap in a window close by. . . . The line of walnut trees no longer sheltered the country road. . . . Only when I swung the gate into the little Mintonye burying ground could I capture a link with the past. Those who lay beneath the handful of weather-beaten monuments, whatever their lives, had at last attained literally the coveted bed of roses, for the old-fashioned thousand-leaf blossoms had been allowed to spread deep over the graves. They were climbing higher and higher toward the pair of stone doves above the inscribed names of my grandparents. . ."

On August 19, 1974, the Tippecanoe County Historical Society erected a historical marker on the old McCutcheon homesite.

McCUTCHEON'S most famous cartoon, at least to Hoosier readers of the *Chicago Tribune,* is *Injun Summer.*

The cartoon first appeared in 1907 and traditionally appears each October in the *Tribune,* in color. It shows an old man sitting on a log, a small boy standing beside him, looking through the autumn haze across a rail fence to the shocks of corn in a distant field. He appears to be saying in part: "You jest come out here tonight when the moon is hangin' over the hill off yonder an' the harvest fields is all swimmin' in the moonlight, an' you can see the Injuns and the tepees jest as plain as kin be."

As to its creation, McCutcheon said: "There was . . . little on my young horizon in the middle seventies beyond corn and Indian traditions. Thirty years later, while groping in the early fall for an idea, it required only a small effort of imagination to see spears and tossing feathers in the tasseled stalks, tepees through the smoky haze; and I evolved *Injun Summer.* Certainly this cartoon of mine about which I have heard most goes back to my earliest childhood, long before I even knew what a cartoon was."

THE LIFETIME association and friendship between McCutcheon and George Ade began during their college days at Purdue University.

McCutcheon describes his first meeting with Ade: "Down in front among the higher classmen I very early noted a delicately modeled face, strangely clean-cut and refined among its more rugged corn-fed neighbors. I found myself fascinated by this cameo profile. Its owner, I eventually learned, was named George Ade. But in those lowly days I could only admire from afar. How could I have presumed to dream that there might come a time when 'Ade and McCutcheon' had as natural a connection as 'ham and eggs'. . . . I was shy and scared and appeared to myself in comparison hopelessly green and awkward, like a puppy who has been taken into a family and doesn't yet know if he is to be kept, ready to like everybody but too timid to make friends."

"A BELIEF I've had for a long time is that it does not matter where one is, it's wholly a matter of what one does while there that makes life interesting. Imagination is the hand-maiden of adventure, and when aided by enterprise, no life can be wholly dull."

DURING THE PERIOD that he was doing a daily cartoon for the *Tribune,* he was also engaged in lecturing. In *Drawn From Memory,* he relates some of his frustrations and experiences:

"I never became sufficiently acclimated to the lecture platform to escape certain agonies. It meant doing a cartoon ahead for the paper, sometimes a strain. Too, there would be a long, tiresome ride in a superheated day coach and an arrival in the early darkness of a winter night on a wind-swept platform of a small-town station. This would be followed by a ride in a rickety bus up to a hotel where commercial travelers eyed me with gloomy suspicion and wondered what 'line' I was carrying. . . .

"I delivered my chalk talk so often that I came to know the good parts and the dull parts.

When I told about the little dog . . . there was a hushed house, not even a cough. When I went on to the salient points about what governs a cartoonist in his work, there was an immediate wavering of attention. . . .

"Once however, when I was in this section of my talk . . . I became conscious of a sudden wave of interest that swept the house. People were sitting bolt upright in rapt attention, and I couldn't understand it. I hoped that at last my serious message had come into its own, but, a little later, it developed that a cat had walked out on the stage and was marching and countermarching behind me. There is nothing like an earnest cat to enliven a discourse. . . .

"Another time I did drive part of the way, fourteen miles to reach a town in northern Indiana, and I arrived nearly an hour late. While I was giving my lecture, the driver got drunk and when we started back he got lost. It was a lonely drive, groping in the darkness of a silent country road at midnight, but somehow we finally made a distant railway station. A week later a farmhouse on this same lonely road was burned and the world was electrified by the revelation of the famous Gunness murder farm. I might quite easily have gone in there to inquire the way, in which case I might not have had the opportunity to lecture any more.

"I never really liked lecturing anyhow. I knew

I had the power of drawing people but I never had any confidence in my ability to entertain them once they were out in front of me. . ."

McCUTCHEON'S national prominence as a political cartoonist began in 1876 when he was sent to St. Louis to cover the Republican National Convention. During the ensuing McKinley-Bryan presidential campaign, to fill up an empty space in a cartoon, he inserted "a harmless-looking little dog" which he continued to show in subsequent cartoons. Readers began to inquire as to the significance of this dog that "sometimes looked surprised and incredulous." The volume of letters increased showing special concern for this dog. One of the cartoons showed Mr. Cleveland accidently rocking on the dog's tail which brought hundreds of letters "suggesting remedies." The following day "when the dog appeared with no visible sign of damage beyond a neat bandage, there was general rejoicing." McCutcheon began to be disturbed by the interest in the dog and no comments about the political import of his cartoons and he was "resolved to get rid of him" by drawing a cartoon in which "a tail was shown disappearing off the side from which floated a little banner saying, 'Farewell forever.' " The response brought thousands of letters, and he had to "bring him back for a time."

HE WON the coveted Pulitzer prize for his cartoons in 1931. While a review of those published represent a pictorial history of the times covered by his work, it was the humorous manner of portrayal of people and events that attracted such a wide following of readers. His type of humor is aptly described by former U.S. Senator, Sam J. Erwin, Jr., of North Carolina, who wrote: "Humor give us smiles, laughter, and gaiety. Humor reveals the roses and hides the thorns. Humor makes our heavy burdens light and smooths the rough spots in our pathways. Humor endows us with the capacity to clarify the obscure, to simplify the complex, to deflate the pompous, to chastise the arrogant, to point a moral, and to adorn a tale."

Prior to the coronation of King Edward VII, when it was indicated in the press that President McKinley might appoint ex-President

Cleveland to be the American representative at the coronation, McCutcheon drew a cartoon showing Cleveland in a boat fishing, "and replying to the President who beckoned from the shore, 'Can't go. Got a bite.' "

AS TO HIS OWN WORK he wrote: "People prefer to be amused rather than reformed. The American people especially, I found, like considerable amiability mixed with its lectures. A pictorial sermon once in ten cartoons is more effective than ten pictorial sermons in a row. . . . This then was the creed which governed my own work. If the one who saw it smiled, its mission was fulfilled; and if, on rare occasions, half a million people smiled in unison, then I felt a great work had been accomplished."

IN THE LATER YEARS of his life he wrote: "When a man looks back over fifty or sixty years—any kind of years—he has certainly acquired a lot of perspective, if nothing else. He sees the mistakes he has made and the lucky breaks he may have had. The entire trend of his life in the early formative period has hinged upon certain decisions he has taken, good or bad."

Nine

THOMAS RILEY MARSHALL (1854–1925), born in North Manchester, Indiana, became the twenty-sixth Governor of the State of Indiana in 1909. He was Vice-President of the United States from 1913 to 1921, during the administration of President Woodrow Wilson.

While the names and accomplishments of vice-presidents are soon forgotten, this amiable Hoosier escaped a similar fate by an inspired observation that came to him during a dull debate in the United States Senate on the needs of the country. He said: "What this country needs is a good five-cent cigar."

Other samples of his now forgotten keen wit and delightful humor are as follows:

"**Y**ES, ANCESTRY is a good thing. Few people can get along without it. It seems to be an absolute household necessity."

"MY GRANDFATHER was one of the pioneers and path-finders. He came to Indiana when it was a primeval forest. He had only youth, a stout heart, a sharp ax, a young wife and courage."

"MY FATHER, looking up through the leaves of an almost impenetrable forest, first saw the stars. He was one of nine children all of whom were taught to work."

"I NEVER KNEW my grandparents on my mother's side. She and they were Pennsylvania born, and her humorous side led her to tell me that they trekked across the Allegheny Mountains and settled in Ohio for the reason that the county in Pennsylvania in which they lived had only four families and they were inter-marrying until there was danger that some man would have an imbecile for an ancestor."

"I HAVE MET nearly all of the great men and women of America who have been prominent in the last forty years; I have seen and conversed with a great many of the illustrious ones from across the sea, and I do not hesitate to place the wreath upon the tomb where rest the ashes of my father and my mother."

93

"I HAVE NO REASON for doing so, but I do believe that human success or human failure is about ten per cent heredity and ninety per cent environment; but I have also another theory, and that is that what the world knows as a bad environment may act as a stimulus to a man for the bettering of his condition."

"A WIFE of a candidate for the Congress of the United States accompanied her husband in his campaign. She had been told that the way to make votes was to manifest a deep interest in children. So, one day, when they were at the home of a prominent Democrat, the wife came in, bearing in her arms a baby boy suffering with hydrocephalus. Awake to the opportunity of the occasion, and unaware of the disease, she exclaimed: 'My! What a head!' "

"WHAT WE KNOW about things that we know nothing about is the most remarkable part of our mental equipment and our education. The less we know the surer we are of our conclusions. It is only the man who has made a thorough study of a subject who hesitates to express an unqualified, absolutely certain opinion."

"IT IS FAR BETTER to have less learning and more moral character in the practice of the law than it is to have great learning and no morals."

"INDEED, this has been the law of my life: To give away gladly and joyfully to anybody who wanted it, anything I did not want myself."

"A WEDDING CEREMONY was performed by a justice of the peace who had just been inducted into office.

"He asked the bridegroom whether he took this woman to be his lawfully wedded wife, without relief from valuation and appraisement laws, and upon an affirmative answer he asked the bride whether she took this man to be her lawfully wedded husband, without benefit of clergy, and upon her nodding her head in assent, he concluded the service by pronouncing them husband and wife, 'in the name of the State of Indiana, Whitley County!'"

"OF COURSE, it is an utterly foolish thing for one man to say what he would have done if he had been in another man's place, at another time. . . . I have always thought that if I had been Adam in the Garden of Eden I would not have eaten the apple—but I do not know. I never saw Eve, and for aught I know, had I been there, instead of merely taking a bite I might have endeavored to consume the entire crop."

"THERE IS a quite current belief that if a man steals enough he can go scot-free; that it is only the moderate-minded thief who ever gets into trouble."

"IN AUDITING the records of an elderly township trustee, the examiners from the State Board of Accounts were puzzled by an entry of a receipt in the Road Fund. When asked to explain the entry he told them that he had to buy a road scraper. Several salesmen called upon him and he finally concluded the purchase with a young salesman who had come to see him by train. As he boarded the train to leave and shook hands with the trustee he left in his hand a twenty-dollar bill. When asked to explain the salesman replied, 'Why, you blamed old fool, that's graft!' The trustee told the examiners that, 'As I knew it did not belong to me, I just put it in the Road Fund and entered it on the books as graft.' "

"MY FATHER thought it would be a good thing for me to keep a record each night of the things that impressed me during the day, and so when I was about ten years of age he gave me a little diary. I remember that on the evening of the first of January, after carefully pondering over my day, I recorded the fact that we had had buckwheat cakes and sausage for breakfast, roast turkey, cranberry sauce and sweet potatoes for dinner. With this record I was compelled to stop, for there seemed to be nothing else in the day that was worth recording for future generations. On the second day I cut the entry in two by the simple announcement that we had buckwheat cakes and sausage while the cold weather lasted. And this is all of the diary I ever kept."

"THE OVERHEAD of the American people would be reduced about ten per cent if in all the walks of life speeches were merely heard and were not printed and circulated. The only person I ever heard of who really liked them, was a hermit in Arkansas who is said to have written inquiring whether they had any more speeches about dead congressman; that if there was anything in the world about which he liked to read, it was a dead congressman."

"I HAVE ALWAYS had a friendly feeling for Andrew Jackson. There is a story to the effect that he was one day informed that a certain Whig official should not be removed and a Democrat placed in his stead; that the Whig was essential to good public service. Whereupon Jackson is reported to have replied; 'If there be an office in the Republic that a Democrat can not fill, let's abolish the office.' "

Ten

HERB SHRINER (1918–1970), was born at To-
ledo, Ohio. When four years of age his family
moved to Fort Wayne, Indiana. He was later to
remark, "Yes, I was born in Ohio all right, but
the family moved to Indiana as soon as they
heard about it."

He first began performing in public as a member of a harmonica band, playing at barn dances,
church socials, fraternal gatherings and later following the vaudeville circuit. His first important
personal appearance came in the fall of 1946 at
the Shubert Theatre in Philadelphia as a member
of the broadway musical, Inside U.S.A., starring
Beatrice Lillie and Jack Haley. He appeared on
the program as "The Guy From Indiana." His
popularity on tour with this broadway musical
earned him an opportunity to later substitute for
Arthur Godfrey on the CBS television show, Talent Scouts. His subsequent monologue appear-

ances on radio and television made him a national celebrity to millions.

Famous writers and critics of his day praised his talent. Jerome Beatty: "Herb is actually one of the folks he talks about, straight from the cracker barrel in the crossroads store." Gene Cook: "Herb simply stands there and talks, but his monologues wander on, punctuated and finally ended by whip-snapping twists of pure idiocy. Shriner gets most of his material from Indiana, from the childhood he spent there, from fond if off-beat memories of curious characters and listless little towns." Peter Ordway: "He is one of the greatest natural comedians in America." Ralph Major, Jr.: "Many quite bluntly say that no one like him has been around since the late Will Rogers. For old-timers agree that no successor has captured so well Rogers' talent for coining timely yet timeless quips. Shriner's wry comments on people's foibles and his deliberately underplayed anecdotes should fit tomorrow's world as well as today's."

A headline in The New York Times on Saturday, April 25, 1970, announced the death of Herb Shriner, "the homespun humorist," and his wife in an automobile accident.

The following selections about "the folks back home" were gleaned from various newspaper and magazine accounts of his life, and from the personal recollection of a performance before The Indiana Society of Chicago.

104

"*T*HE TOWN was full of live wires—trouble was, they weren't hooked up to anything."

"THERE WASN'T MUCH to do around home on Saturdays except to drop down to the barbershop and watch haircuts."

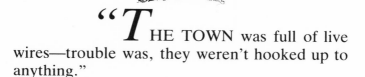

"WHEN I was a kid, I remember how my grandfather used to trim the window in his little store. All he did was to wash the cat and put in some clean flypaper."

"WE HAD a burglar in our town. Everyone knew him as Joe the burglar. We knew he was burgling. We didn't mind much 'cause we knew he was a local boy, and it kept the money in town."

"AROUND HOME a kid would usually get his suit handed down to him from his father; then, when the kid got through with it, he'd hand it down to the next kid. In fact, if a suit had a few kids left in it, the family wouldn't throw the suit away; they'd go ahead and have the kids. It got so a woman'd hate to see a good suit come into the family."

"I REMEMBER a sheriff we once had. He was honest as the day is long, but of course when it got dark, you had to watch him."

"OUR MAIL was always slow back home. It was the postmaster's fault—he was a slow reader. We didn't mind him reading the mail so much, but we got peeved when he started answering it too."

"WE HAD a salesman down home. This guy used to sell lightnin' rods until one night he got caught in a storm with a lot of samples."

"MY HOME TOWN had one big trouble. Not enough git-up-and-go. Actually, we'd get up, but there wasn't anyplace to go."

"ONE OF MY old friends down home was a railroad switchman. He was kinda hard of hearing and the trains would sneak through on him. So he took to sittin' on the track. He's gone now."

"NOT TO BE outdone by the larger cities, our town put in a lot of one-way streets and all the cars was trapped outside of town. The trouble was they forgot to make any streets comin' back."

"WE DIDN'T EVEN have a statue around there. We were gonna put up a statue for a local fella who had gone off and got famous and then he never came back so we couldn't find out who he was."

"WE HAD a hotel in town. It wasn't much, but at least it had a bridal suite. That was the room with a lock on the door."

"A FELLA down home quit his job. We was kinda worried. His folks was worried too, so they got him into politics where he wouldn't be noticed. He was honest as could be. If he got bought off, he stayed bought off. He wasn't shifty."

"DOWN HOME there was only one player in the pinochle parlor who knew how to shuffle. Unless you sat at his table, you'd keep getting the same cards back."

"AT HOME nobody ever bought many papers. You knew what everybody else was doin'. You'd just buy a paper once in a while to see if they had got caught at it."

"IN OUR TOWN everybody used to vote. Why, one friend of mine used to come twenty miles to town just to vote. He never seemed to mind the trip, though. Said it was the only money he made all year."

"WE HAD A sheriff back home. Pretty heavy drinker, he was. We used to kid him about his bloodshot eyes. One day he says to us—he was feelin' worse than usual that day—and he says, 'If you think my eyes is bloodshot, you ought to see 'em from this side.' "

"TAKE THE MAYOR of my home town. He made a campaign speech and said, 'Friends, I sure am proud of you citizens in this town and all the things you stand for.' And believe me, we sure stood for plenty."

"WE HAD a resort, too. A resort is a place where a lot of girls are looking for husbands, and a lot of husbands are looking for girls."

"BACK HOME the community's wealthiest citizens got rich after he invented a dog food that tasted like a postman's leg."

"EVERY TOWN always has a fellow who keeps getting himself messed up. Like the Peter's boy we had back home. He painted the church steeple from the bottom up. He was up there three days waiting for the paint to dry.

112

We had to slingshot apples up to him to keep him going. I don't like apples much."

"WE NEVER KNEW we had anybody who could act in the family. But one day folks back home found an old picture in the attic. Thought it was my uncle on an ornate stage. Well, it inspired me, you might say. Decided to get into show business. Anyhow, it wasn't until years later that I got a good look at that picture. Turned out he wasn't an actor at all. His number had just been called in a turkey raffle. That's how he got on the stage. Well, anyway, by then it was too late to stop me."

"NEVER FORGET the day my daughter, Indy, was born. There I was, pacing up and down the floor. Nothing to read or anything. Well, it sure was tough. I'm certainly glad the baby was a girl—so she'll never have to go through the same ordeal I did."

"WE JUST HAD a little school at home. So small they had to put all the little kids in the front row so they could see. Big ones sat in the rear. When you got bigger, you got moved back. And when you were too big even for the back row, you were graduated. Couldn't flunk you; they'd have to set the big boys in the front row again."

"IN THE AMUSEMENT PARK back home we had a pretty special roller-coaster everybody liked to ride. Well, the thing started to get along in years. First thing we knew the big bumps started to get smoothed down. Then nobody's got on that roller-coaster any more. Was like riding a streetcar."

114

"A BOY went into the drug store down home and asked for ten cents worth of asafetida and told the druggist to charge it to his father. The druggist said, 'What's your father's name.' The boy replied, 'Schermerhorn.' The druggist said, 'You take it for nothing, I ain't going to spell asafetida and Schermerhorn for no dime.' "

"WE HAD A couple of fellows in politics back home that went down to Washington. We didn't think they was doin' nothing. Actually they weren't, but they were so good at it, you couldn't tell."

"THERE WAS A FELLOW down home who wasn't too bright as a kid. When they gave him those intelligence tests in school, he'd always try to put the square peg in the round holes. Funny thing is, he could do it—he was stronger than most kids."

"ONE of the Crumpacker kids at the age of fifteen went to the courthouse to get a marriage license. When told he was too young, he replied, 'Just give me a beginner's permit.' "

"WHEN I TOLD my home folks these stories, they was just bored. Like, I guess, giraffe jokes ain't funny in Africa. I tried changing—saying these things happened in Ohio. It didn't do any good. Ohio ain't a funny state. There's only three funny states—Indiana, Texas and Brooklyn."

116

118

Eleven

GABRIEL GODFROY (1834–1910), was born in Blackford County, Indiana, the son of Francois Godfroy, a Miami war chief and trader, half French and half Indian.

Through him, as one of the last survivors of this original tribe in Indiana, much of the Miami Indian lore and history has been preserved.

ONE OF GABRIEL'S wives was a grand-daughter of Frances Slocum, the famed Indian girl in Indiana history known as "The Lost Sister of Wyoming."

In 1778, Frances, the five year old daughter

of a Quaker family living along the Susquehanna River in Pennsylvania, was torn from her mother's arms and carried away by three Delaware Indians, while her father was away putting up hay. She was adopted and reared by this tribe and married a Miami chief. Years later they settled on the Mississinewa River near Peru, Indiana, at what was known as "The Deaf Man's Village." Fifty-nine years later she was reunited with two brothers and a sister whose long search for her ended when they came from Pennsylvania to Peru. However she continued to remain on her farm where she died in 1847, and where a monument is erected in her memory.

A SIZEABLE ESTATE in land came to Gabriel upon the death of his father, but through the press of white settlement and prolonged and costly litigation, the greater part was lost. Though he had paid taxes on considerable land in 1872 and 1876, he was denied the right to vote. However in the national election of 1880, when turned away with the remark, "You can't vote you damned Indian" he chased the election clerks with a war club and while they were gone "proceeded to mark over 200 ballots for James A. Garfield."

JACOB PIATT DUNN, author of *True Indian Tales* and *Indiana and Indianans,* said of him: "He was an amiable, honorable gentleman, who bore adversity bravely, and was universally respected. . . . He had no schooling. However he had a bright mind and a fine memory. His excellence as an interpreter was due to his general information and the fact that he knew English so well he could think in it as well as in Miami."

E. W. LAMB, author of *Indian Lore,* and Jacob Piatt Dunn spent many hours with Gabriel, recording and preserving for future generations Miami Indian lore, legends, meaning of words and names. They were also able to preserve some of the eloquent utterances of Miami chiefs such as the prayer of Chief Yellow Lark: "Oh Great Spirit, whose voice I hear in the winds, and whose breath gives life to all the world, hear me. I come before You, one of Your many children. I am small and weak. I need Your strength and wisdom. Let me walk in beauty and make my eyes ever behold the red and purple sunset. Make my hands respect the things You have made, my ears sharp to hear Your voice. Make me wise, so that I may know the things You have taught my people, the lesson You have hidden in every leaf and rock. I seek strength not to be superior to my brothers, but to be able to fight my greatest enemy—myself."

GABRIEL delivered a talk on June 16, 1907, at the Tippecanoe Battle Ground, near Lafayette, in which he said in part:

"My Kind Friends. I have got no learning, I have no education. I can not talk to you like the white man. I can only tell you of things that I have seen and that have been told to me.

"My father lived near Peru, Indiana. I was

born there. I can not read or write. When a little boy I passed through Lafayette on my way to a Catholic school at Vincennes. I could only use the Miami language. We went from Lafayette to Vincennes on a packet boat. I was only six months there when my mother got homesick for me and I went home in a sleigh. I went home and went to hunting squirrels and never went to school any more.

"My people, the Miamis made peace with the whites in Washington's time and we never violated it. My people did not take part in the battle of Tippecanoe. If they had the result would have been different for it was very close anyhow. The red men made their treaties and kept them but the white men did not. Whenever they were dissatisfied they would give us a little money and make a new treaty.

"I am a Miami. My father was half Indian and half French and his name was Francois Godfroy. I was born in 1834. The Miamis were the stoutest and swiftest of all the Indians. Indian always keeps his word; white men don't. White men very uncertain.

"I used to own a good deal of land. I have only forty-eight acres now. I was cheated out of my property by the white man. I have had nineteen children and three wives. Indians believe in big families like President Roosevelt. My second wife was a granddaughter of Frances Slocum. . ."

124

Twelve

ELBERT M. ANTRIM (1885–1961), was born in Rensselaer, Indiana. His mother died when he was a small boy and he was raised by other members of the family. His life story was a prototype of the poor Hoosier boy, born on a farm or in a small town, who later achieved an eminent executive position in the business world of a large city.

He attended the Rensselaer schools. Following graduation from high school in 1903, he completed a short secretarial business course which enabled him to be employed as a secretary to an executive of the Equitable Life Insurance Company. Shortly thereafter he became clerk of the General Freight Office of the Burlington Railroad.

In 1917 he replied to a want ad in the Chicago Tribune *and was hired to "establish a traffic department" for The Tribune Company. From Traf-*

125

fic Manager, he advanced to Assistant to the President, Assistant Business Manager, and Business Manager in 1944, which position he held until his retirement in 1954. During this period he was a member "of most of the Tribune subsidiaries and affiliated companies." As a member of the board of governors of the American Newspaper Publishers Association he "contributed much to the progress of the newspaper industry."

During his years with The Tribune Company he had a distinguished record of service with many professional organizations and companies. He was chairman of the Harbors and Waterways Commission, member of the executive committee of the Chicago Association of Commerce, member of the advisory board of Inland Waterways Corporation, and one of the organizers and directors of the Mutual Broadcasting System.

*A*S THE BUSINESS manager of a large metropolitan newspaper he gained the friendship of famous editors, authors, reporters, cartoonists and politicians. One of

126

them wrote: "His kindness and understanding and wisdom splash over onto anyone that comes in contact with him."

In looking back over his life he said, "That no matter how disappointments and hurts seem unjust and unreasonable, in time you learn that the object of man's life is to make something of himself in spite of all the hazards and set-backs of living."

WHEN ANTRIM RETIRED in 1954, Col. Robert R. McCormick, editor and publisher of the *Chicago Tribune,* ordered an editorial written entitled, "A MAN NAMED ANTRIM," lauding his years of service. In response to its publication Antrim wrote a letter to Col. McCormick, in Florida, on June 22, 1954, reading in part as follows:

"When I read a laudatory obituary I always think it is a shame that the poor man is not here to read the nice things said about him. The wonderful editorial about my retirement in yesterday's Tribune does not have this objectionable feature. It allows me to pleasantly savor those kind thoughts while I am more or less possessed of all my faculties.

"Don Maxwell boasts that he is the only man from Greencastle, Indiana, who ever became managing editor of the *Chicago Tribune*. Pete Green brags that he is the only native of Ligonier, Indiana, who ever became governor of Illinois twice. Now I can truthfully say, with the possible exception of Charlie Halleck, I am the only guy from Rensselaer who ever had a *Tribune* editorial written about him.

"My typical Hoosier false modesty will not permit me to question the veracity of the editorial. However, I assure you it will not be the cause of any excessive egotism on my part. I learned my lesson in that regard some years ago when it was emphatically demonstrated to me that if I ever found myself floating on the clouds of self-esteem I could quickly get my feet back on the ground by simply paying a visit to my own home town.

"This is what happened: I went back to Rensselaer to attend a funeral of an old family friend and an esteemed citizen. The whole county was there, filling the house and overflowing on the lawn. Someone told me Mrs. John Greenfield had expressed a desire to see me. I remembered that when I was a small child she was a very old lady. I found her holding court seated in a rocking chair on the lawn. When I shook hands with her she said, 'Well,

well, you are Jim Antrim's boy. I knew you when you wore long dresses. I knew your father. I knew your grandfather. Where are you located now?'

"I told her 'Chicago,' and then waited eagerly for her to ask me what I was doing so that I could then really go to town in explaining how I had gone up in the world and what a perfect example I was of local boy makes good. To my consternation her next statement was 'Well, I hope you have steady employment.' Those folks in Rensselaer can really put you in your place.

"I went back home one time to attend a high school alumni reunion. The toastmaster made a big point of introducing the distinguished guests.

"The degree of distinction seemed to be measured by the distance each one traveled to attend the function. I got scant notice because I had traveled only 72 miles on the Monon from Chicago, suburb of Rensselaer. The individual who got the loudest applause came all the way from Denver, Colorado. George Ade, whom everyone knew, was not even mentioned. He came only 18 miles from his farm near Brook."

SELECTED BIBLIOGRAPHY

Ade, John. *Newton County.* Indianapolis: The Bobbs-Merrill Company, 1911.

Banta, R.E. *Hoosier Caravan.* Bloomington: Indiana University Press, 1951.

Dickey, Marcus. *The Youth of James Whitcomb Riley.* Indianapolis: The Bobbs-Merrill Company, 1919.

Dunn, Jacob Piatt. *Indiana and Indianans.* 5 vol. 3 biographical. Chicago and New York: The American Historical Society, 1919.

Dunn, Jacob Piatt. *True Indian Stories.* Indianapolis: Sentinel Printing Co., 1908.

Erwin, Sam J. Jr., *Humor of A Country Lawyer.* Chapel Hill and London: University of North Carolina Press, 1983.

Gresham, Matilda. *Life of Walter Quintin Gresham.* Chicago: Rand McNally & Company, 1919.

Kelley, Fred C. *George Ade, Warmhearted Satirist.* Indianapolis-New York: The Bobbs-Merrill Company, 1947.

131

Kunitz, Stanley J. *Authors Today and Yesterday*. New York: The H.W. Wilson Company, 1933.

Lamb, E.W. *Indian Lore*. Indiana: Light & Life Press, 1964.

Marshall, Thomas R. *Recollections of Thomas Riley Marshall*. Indianapolis: The Bobbs-Merrill Company, 1925.

McCutcheon, John T. *Cartoons by McCutcheon*. Chicago: A.C. McClurg & Co., 1903.

McCutcheon, John T. *Drawn From Memory*. Indianapolis and New York: The Bobbs-Merrill Company, Inc., 1950.

Peckman, Howard H. *Indiana A Bicentennial History*. W.W. Norton & Company, Inc., 1978.

Phelps, William Lyon. *Letters of James Whitcomb Riley*. Indianapolis: The Bobbs-Merrill Company, 1930.

Riley, James Whitcomb. *Sketches In Prose*. Indianapolis: The Bowen-Merrill Co., 1894.

Schultz, L.W. *Indian Lore*. Indiana: Light & Life Press, 1964.

Spink, J.G. Taylor. *Judge Landis and Twenty-Five Years of Baseball*. New York: Thomas Y. Crowell Company, 1947.

Wallace, Lew. *An Autobiography*. Completed by Susan Elston Wallace and Mary Hannah Kraut. 2 vol. New York: Harper and Brothers, 1906.

Wilson, William E. *Indiana: A History*. Bloomington and London: Indiana University Press, 1966.

The Author

John S. Blue was born at Rensselaer, Indiana, on December 31, 1915, one of six children of Philip Roy Blue and Adelaide (Phillips) Blue. He is a lifetime resident of Jasper County, a rural farm community in the northwestern corner of Indiana. He is a descendant of John Blue I (1691–1770), one of the earliest pioneer settlers of Hampshire County, in the Allegheny Mountains of Virginia, now West Virginia.

His early years were spent on a small farm near the town of Wheatfield where he graduated from high school. He was married to Sarah V. Wright on August 18, 1946.

He has been an abstractor and searcher of land titles for more than thirty-five years. He was President of the Indiana Land Title Association in 1952 and 1953, editor of its first trade publication, and a member of the Board of Governors of the American Land Title Association in 1954 and 1955.

His father was a school teacher, public official, abstractor of land titles, and a country lawyer. Following his retirement, the author and his wife have continued the operation of the Jasper County Abstract Company, founded by his father in 1928.

The Artist

Living in the Indiana Dunes country, Dale Fleming reflects the life around him in realistic paintings that yet show a gentle understanding of people, familiar dune scenes, and places in Colorado.

His sketch book is ever with him, and his friends and his own son, Carl, provide subject matter for many of his portraits.

Mr. Fleming's background includes several years of study at the American Academy of Art in Chicago and with several area artists. He has won awards in numerous shows (Southern Shores, Napanee, Tri Kappa, & Hammond) and taught classes at the Michigan City and Gary Artists leagues as well as exhibiting at a number of galleries in Chicago, different Indiana cities, Michigan and Kentucky. Additionally he has illustrated two children's books for Albert Whitman Company.

His special love is the dunes area where he lives, and his acrylic paintings combine the delicate skill of the water colorist he was with the colors of acrylic paintings.